Poor Tugger's Almanac of Canine Wisdoms

Proverbs...of the pooches, by the pooches, for the pooches

by Jolie Bell

Poor Tugger's Almanac of Canine Wisdoms

Proverbs...of the pooches, by the pooches, for the pooches

Written & Illustrated by Jolie Bell

Book & Cover Layout & Design By Vernon Firestone

ISBN# 0-9774640-0-8

First printing November 2005

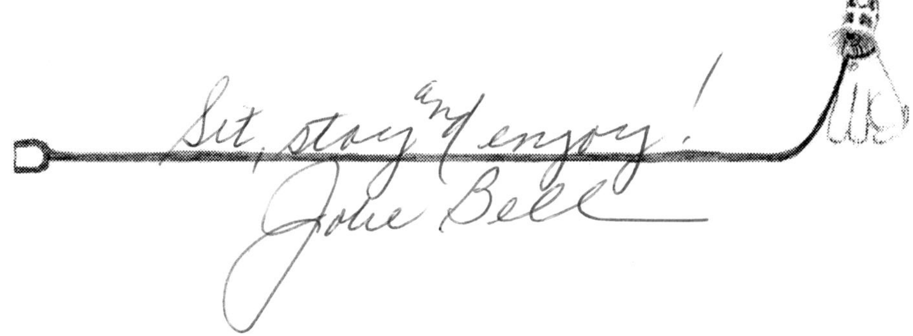

To ____

From ____

Date ____

This book is dedicated to my family
Because they take good care of me.
They're not canine,
But they're all mine.

Love to Steve, Erynn, Christopher, Roman, Auntie & Grandma.
Love and a big hug for George from Granny.
Another thank you to friends for listening and supporting.
A special thank you to Lacey for being born and providing
the reason for getting the whole Tugger thing started.

About Tugger

Hi, I'm Tugger. Welcome to my world. Here I am with my human family. That's Christopher on the left. He scratches my ears real good. Erynn's holding me. She smothers me with people kisses. Steve is my outdoor buddy. I supervise his yard work. My dog-ma, Jolie, keeps me company. I share my innermost thoughts with her.

We had lots of adventures and fun on our great-smelling piece of property in Westerville, Ohio.

I'm glad I was able to bring such joy and fulfillment to their lives. I hope to bring laughter and wisdom to yours!

Jolie and Steve live in Florida now with their loyal companion, Doogie Schnauzer, who supervises Jolie's efforts to preserve the wisdoms of Tugger for future human and canine generations.

ODE TO POOR TUGGER

Alas! Poor Tugger, I knew him well.
He was a dog, though hard to tell.
Nearly human was he
To his friends and family.

Upon a pedestal he did stand,
Revered throughout the land;
Treated like royalty,
Bestowed with loyalty,
His slightest wish was our command.

None could dispute
He was wisest of wise,
Cutest of cute.
For Tug, there was no substitute.

May his wisdom bring
To you and me
A world in which a dog might be
The very greatest living thing.

His praises sing
While worshipping
The exalted one...Poor Tug, the King!

A picture of me is worth a thousand words. A thousand pictures of me would be too cute for words.

Clothes make the man.
An attitude makes the mutt.

Never put off until tomorrow that which you can chew today.

Don't bite the hand that feeds you until the food is all gone.

The family that licks together sticks together.

6

Seek and ye shall find a flea on your behind.

He who laps last laps an empty bowl.

A rolling bone gathers rug fuzz.

Time flies when you're having fun.
Time to fly when you've had too much fun.

10

A watched Rott never soils.

Don't whine over spilled milk.
Just hurry and lick it up
before the mop can pick it up.

Love thy neighbor but breedeth not their poodle.

Desperate times call for desperate beggars.

Cuteness is only fur deep,
but it's often all you really need to get by.

Drool is thicker than water.

Obey thy master...
occasionally.

A man's best friend is a dog. A dog's best friend is a lousy cook.

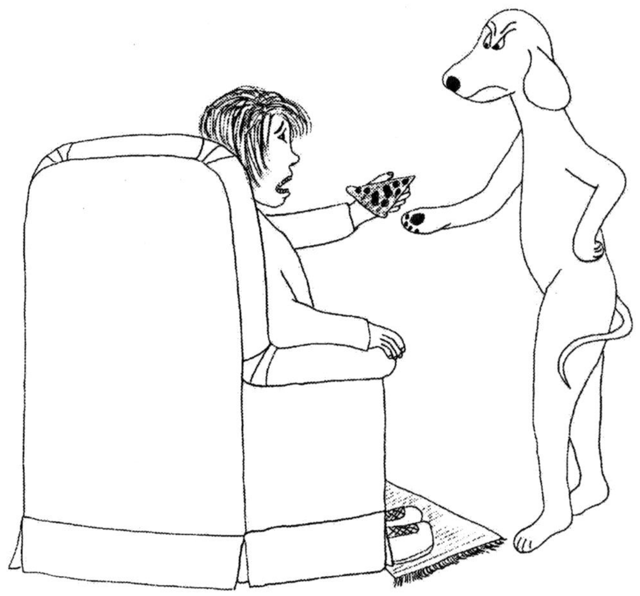

'Tis better to give to your dog than to receive his ire.

A lie stands on one leg, truth on two,
and me on three when I water a tree.

To err is human,
to be forgiven by
your canine is divine.

Once bitten, twice as likely to be shy of dogs.

22

23

When opportunity knocks, yap your head off!

As ye sow wild oats, so shall ye reap a litter.

24

One good breed deserves another.

Is an ounce of raw meat worth a pound from a can?

Don't burn your bitches behind you...
they may be in heat soon.

Time heals all wounds, but lick 'em anyway.
It's tradition.

Fetch as fetch can.

Let thy bones be my bones.

Late to bed, early to rise; to a puppy this applies.

One rotten apple can spoil the whole bunch,
but I'd eat them anyway in one gigantic munch.

A biscuit a day keeps the vet away.
A dozen or so is better I'd say.

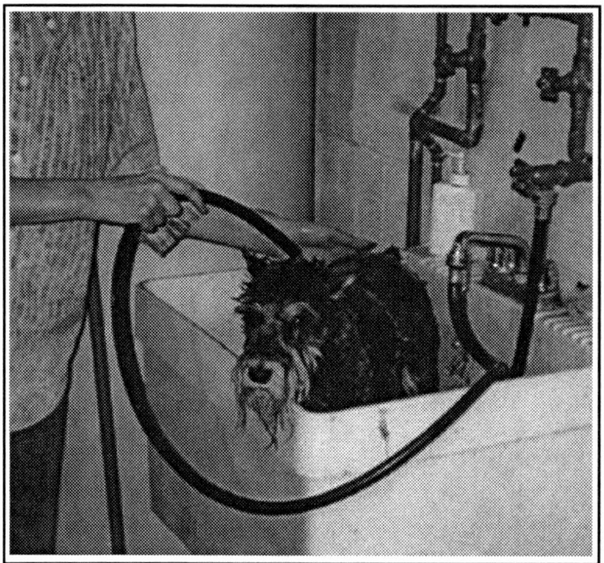

Eat, drink and be merry today
for tomorrow you may have to get a bath.

It takes two to untango me.

It's better to be safe inside a master's home
than to be sorry hounds who have to hunt and roam.

The grass is seldom greener on the other side of the fence
for that's the place I run to when I have incontinence.

He who lieth down with dogs may rise up with fleas.

Fools rush into my territory
where even angels fear to tread.

A bone in the paw
is worth two in the pantry.

Two wrongs on the floor don't make a right good impression.

Hitch your wagger to a star, never to the bumper of your car.

The squeaky whelp
gets the grease.

Slow but steady sets the pace
but will not win the canine race.

If you live in a glass house, better bury your bones.

Don't count your blessings until I'm housebroken.

The pet is mightier than the pen.

Silence may be golden to ye,
but yappy is happy to me.

Fish and visitors stink after three days,
so do my accidents.

Idle paws are boring paws.

Spare the rod
and spoil the pup
so he can really
live it up.

Sticks and stones
may break my bones,
but they'll be just
as tasty.

The way to a dog's heart
is through a hearty snack.

Turn about is fair play,
so turn about
and I'll sniff you out.

Lightning never strikes the same place twice, but I sure do.

All that glitters is the rhinestones on my collar.

A steak well-done is better than, well...none!

Take time to smell the bushes along the way.

Let sleeping dogs lie...wherever they're comfy.

Don't eat to live, live to eat...
table scraps cannot be beat.

If the shoe fits, tear it to shreds.

Familiarity breeds contempt. My master breeds show dogs.

You can lead a pup to paper but you cannot make him wet.

Leave no bone unturned.

The hand that stocks the pantry
rules my world.

Out of the mouths
of babes come crumbs.
Try to lick 'em up before
the vacuum comes.

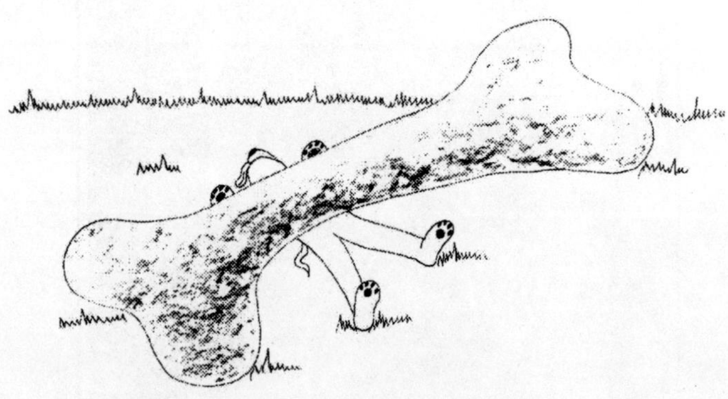

The bigger they are, the harder they fall on me.

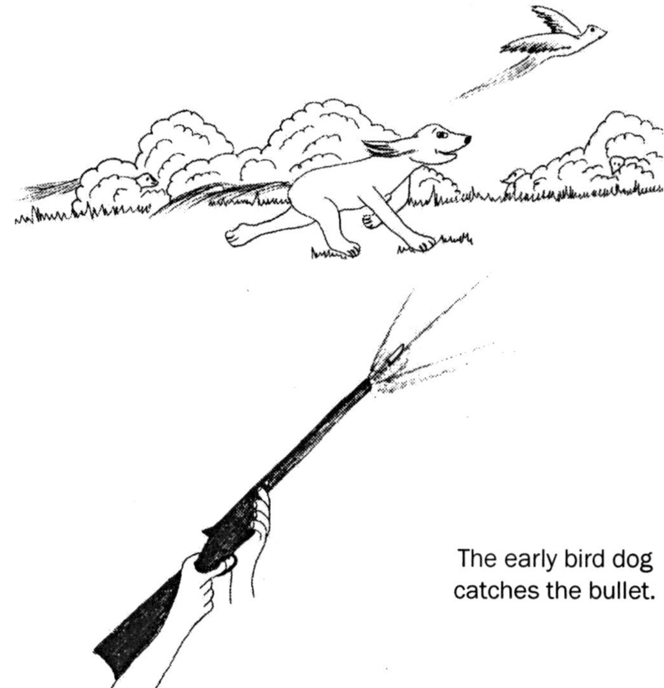

The early bird dog
catches the bullet.

Two's company, three's a litter.

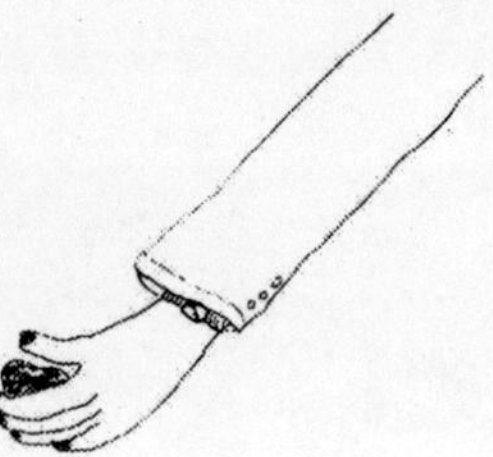

Virtue is it's own reward.
I prefer something a little
more tangible.

Starve a cold, feed a
feverishly hungry pup.

You are what you eat,
that's why I'm such
a treat.

Curiosity killed the cat.
I had absolutely nothing
to do with that.

Walk softly and
carry a big stick.
This is the motto
of Dogcatcher Dick.

Cast ye not the first bone. Save it for your very own.

A nose by any other name smells just the same.

It always makes a lot of sense
to look before you leap a fence.

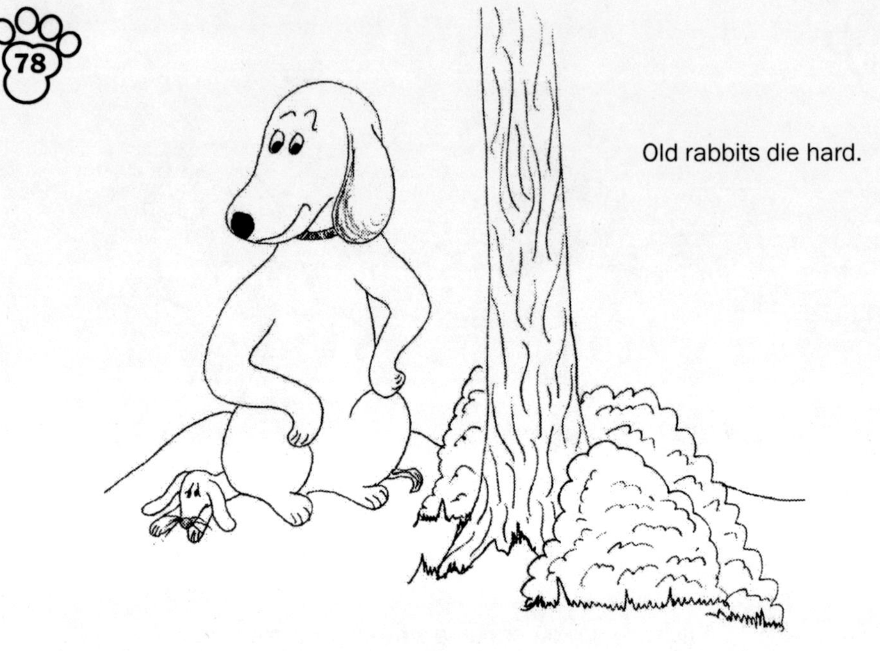

Old rabbits die hard.

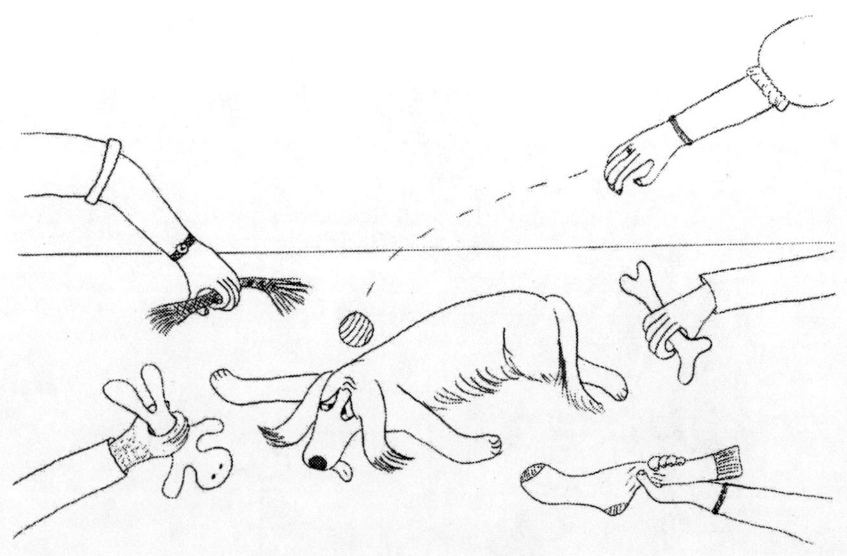

A dog played out is a dog laid out.

Seeing is believing;
peeing is relieving.

See no evil,
hear no evil,
leak no evil.

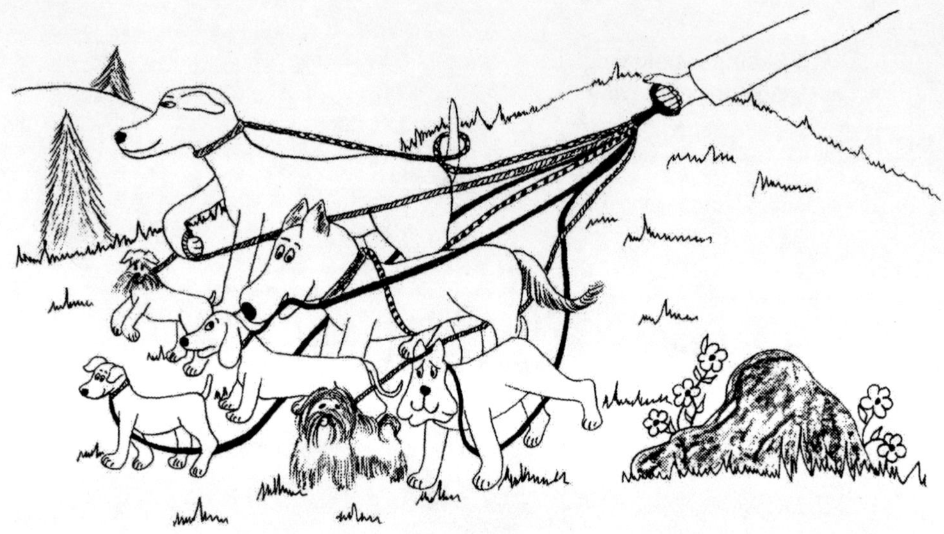

Dogs of a tether walk together.

A dog in need is indeed a dog to feed.

Stick not your nose into
another dog's business.

To thine own whelp be true.

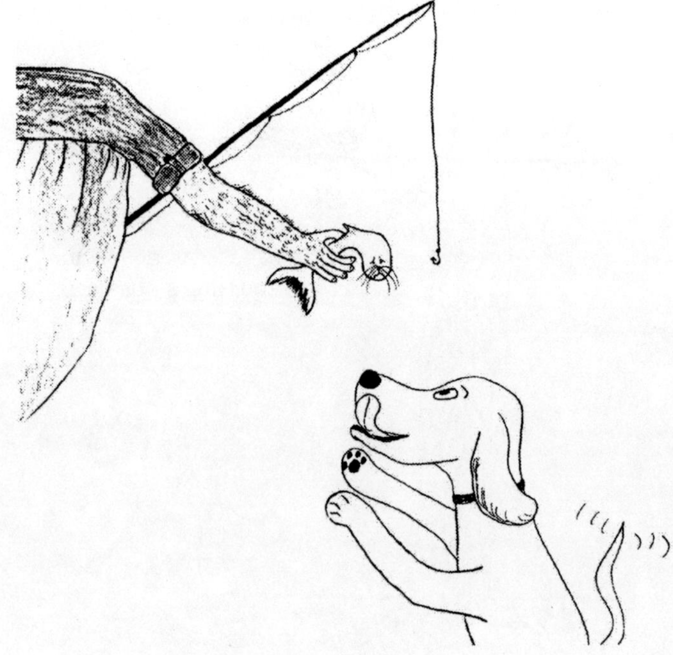

There are plenty of fish in the sea,
but a catfish is the one for me.

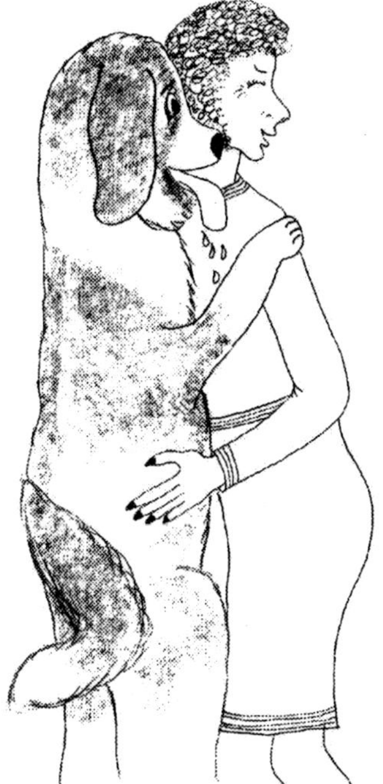

Flattery will get you a lick on the face and almost every other place.

Out of sight, out of mind. Canine translation: If you think I'll be a good boy when you're out of sight, you're out of your mind.

If you play with fire, you'll be burned.
If you play with my toys, I'll be burned.

Strike while the food is hot,
otherwise you may get naught.

90

A word to the wise is sufficient...
and that word is "Grrrrrrrrrrrrrrr!"

Home is where the hound is.

A Spitz in time saves crime.

Misery loves company,
so do I because they always
make such a fuss over me.

Do as I say, not as I doo doo.

All's well that ends my smell.

Ask and ye may receive.
Ask not and ye may receive a swat.

If you want some action, speak louder than words.

Hell hath no fury like a restless pup.

Beggars can't be choosers, but they're more often winners than losers.

Better late than never mate.

No news is good news when I'm finished with it.

Many paws make light work of the neighbor's garden.

Many are called but few have chosen to listen.

No matter who they're from,
nice things in small packages come.

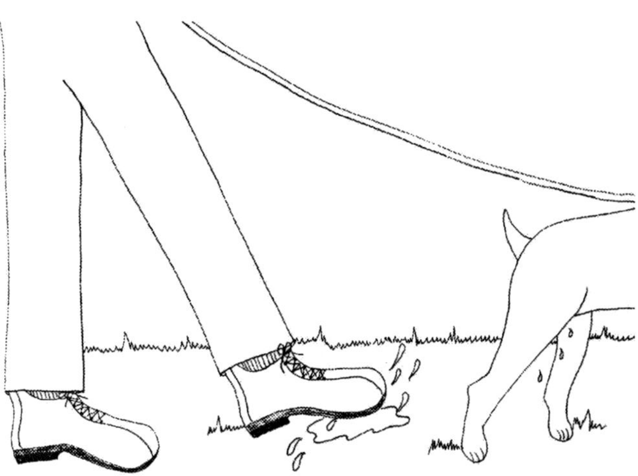

Walk a mile in your shoes.

There's no drool like a cold drool.

Instead of one terrier, the more the merrier.

If at first you do not breed,
try, try again until you can succeed.

It's always darkest before the dawn,
but by then I'll be long gone.

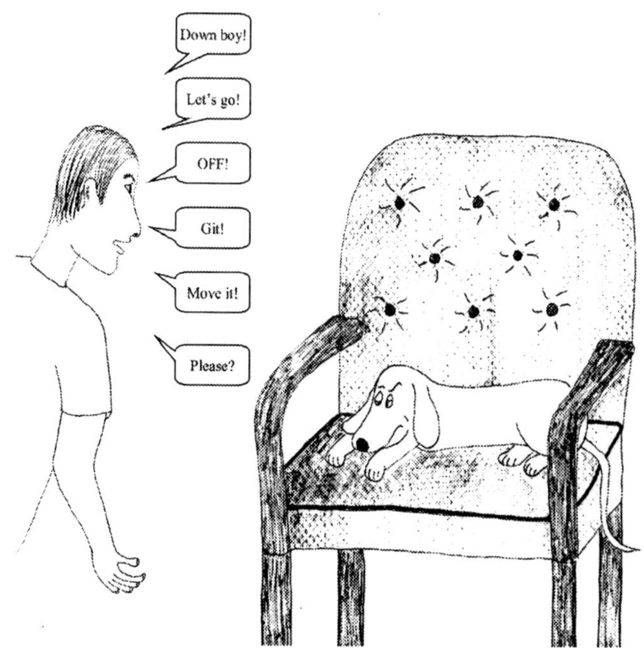

Practice neither what the master preaches
nor anything he beseeches.

All good fleas must come to an end.

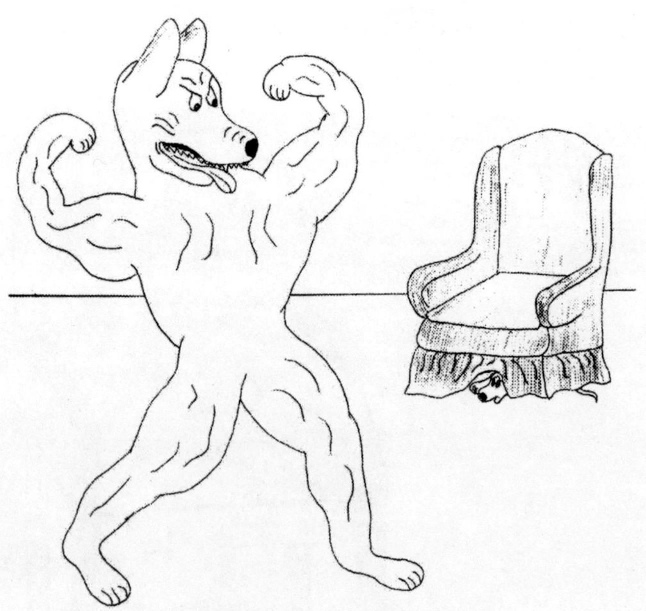

Right makes might.
This makes a frightening sight
that makes me right uptight.

If you can't beat 'em, lie down, roll over and play dead.

Charity begins at the dog pound.

March in like a lion and
come out with a lamb chop.

117

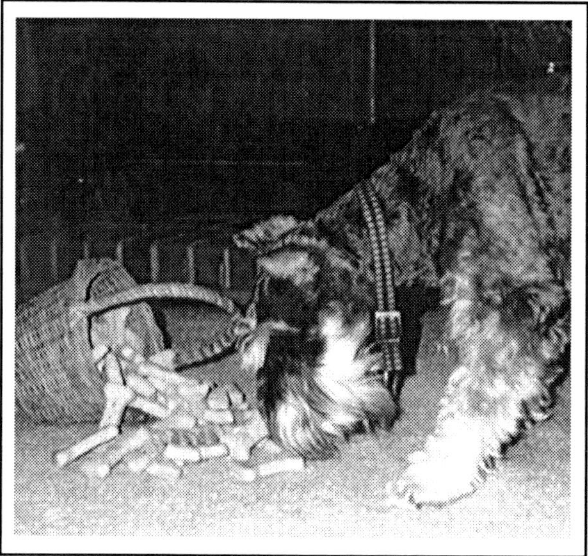

Don't put all your biscuits
eggsclusively in one basket.

A dog is known by the company he keeps...away.

118

All work and no play makes Jack a good watch dog.

Where there's a will, there's a way
to get another treat.

120

Give a feller enough rope,
he'll hang himself up.

There's a time and
a place for everything.
Now is the time so place
me outdoors.

123

Take things one step at a time in my territory.

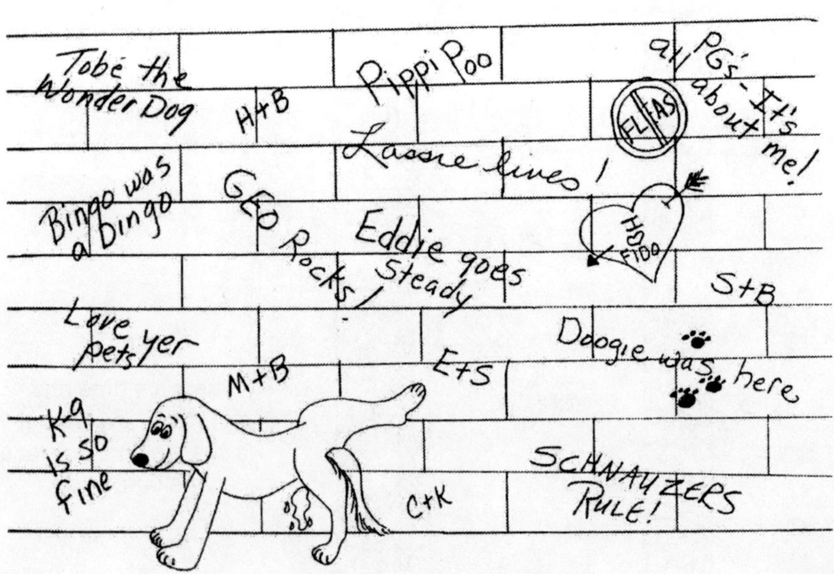

The handwriting is on the wall.
I'll just add my John Hancock.

124

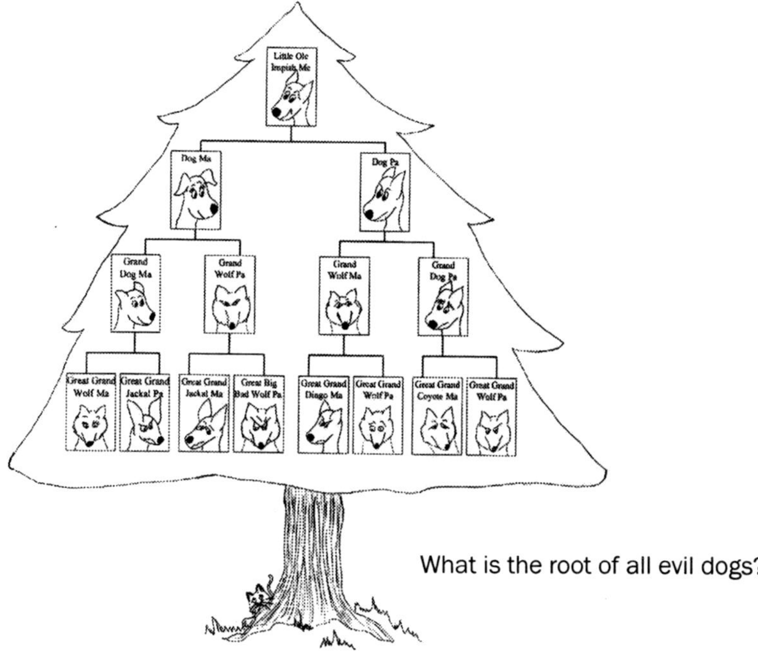

What is the root of all evil dogs?

A dog's bark is worse than its bite...yeah right!

He who hesitates has lost his plates.

A canine's work is never done
until he's sniffed out everyone.

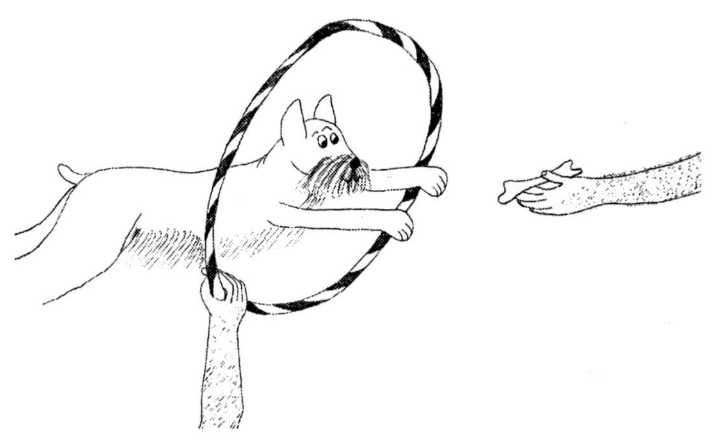

Practice makes perfect sense
as long as there's a treat involved.

There's no time like the present
for opening a present.

A place for everything and everything in it's place.
Everything in my place is all over the place.

Remember the GOLDEN DROOL: Slobber onto others as you would have them slobber onto you.

133

A doggie's place is with his bone.

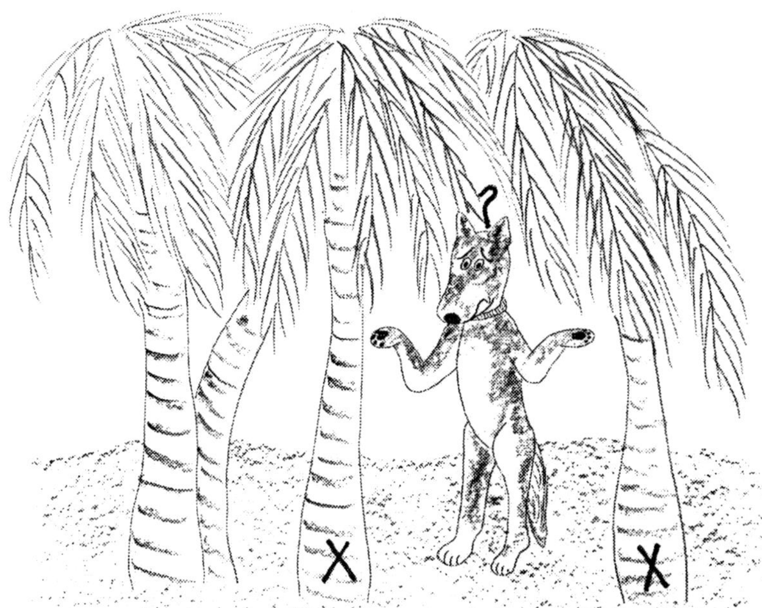

A leopard cannot change his spots; neither can a Shepherd once he's marked them.

134

Dogs cannot live by bread alone.
A balanced diet includes
a large and meaty bone.

Accidents will happen...especially when I get excited.

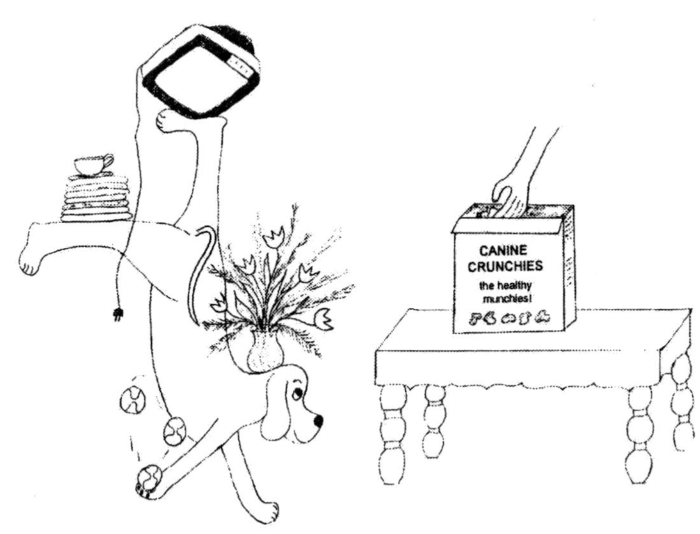

One good trick deserves another treat.

Nothing ventured nothing gained.
Chew forever if you must to
get yourself unchained.

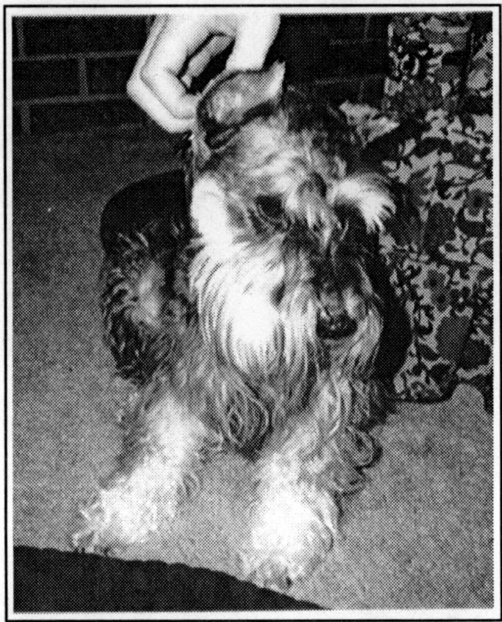

Different folks use different strokes,
but mostly they all scratch behind the ears.

The sincerest form if flattery is imitation.
My form of flattery knows no limitation.

You can have your cake and eat it too
unless I find it before you do.

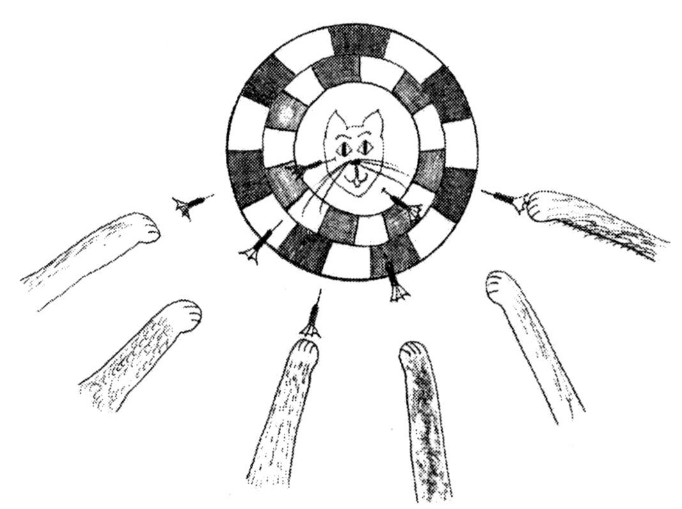

Two dogs are better than one.
One dog is better than none.
Any dog is better than a cat.

143

I hope spring's eternal because it's been
mighty cold out here all winter.

Too many cooks can spoil the mutt, increase his gut
and cause him to lay for the entire day
on his lazy, furry old butt.

145

Shape up or you'll be shipped out to obedience school.

Honestly, the best policy is relaxation.

146

147

The absence of my family makes my heart grow fonder
of that other family over yonder.

What goes around comes around,
but still I can't quite reach it.

149

Little strokes fell great oaks.
How could anyone be so cruel?

Haste makes waste.
If I had hasted, I might have been wasted.

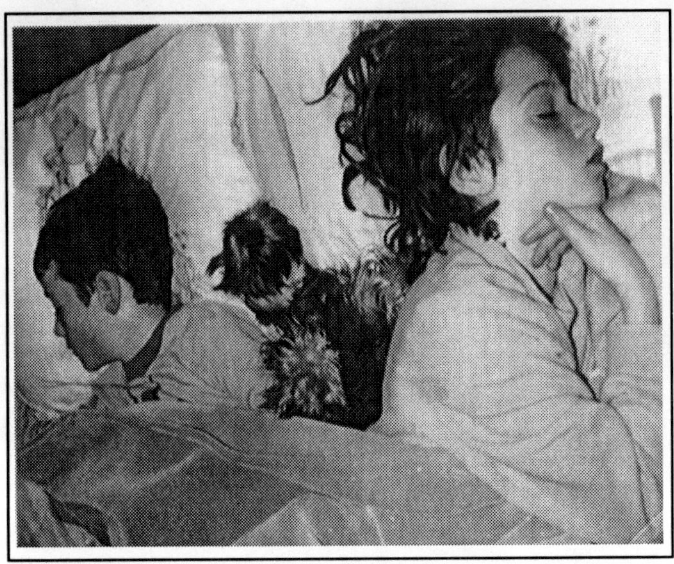

Ignorance is bliss. Bliss is getting away with this.

You never know what you can do until you try.
Sometimes you're better off not knowing.

If you've been a pest, do as we rehearsed...
hope for the best but prepare for the worst.

Like father like son since our family was begun.

155

From a tiny acorn the mighty oak is grown.
As soon as it's big enough, I'll mark it for my own.

Between two stools one falls to the ground.
Let's hope this is true.

Experience is the best teacher for an inquisitive little creature.

Every man has his price, but I can guarantee
that no man will think twice about spending
a fortune for me.

Faith can move mountains...me too!

Fight fire with firedogs.

Every dog has his day. This is mine so stay away.

There's none so deaf as he who cannot hear,
so won't somebody pluck these hairs
out of my ear?

What's bred in the bone comes out in the flesh.
Need I say more?

Something one should never do is bite off
more than one can chew.

165

Every rule has an exception for one of such perfection.

Give credit where credit is due.
I believe this work of art belongs to you.

Let the buyer beware of what lurks under all that hair.

Never give a sucker an even break.

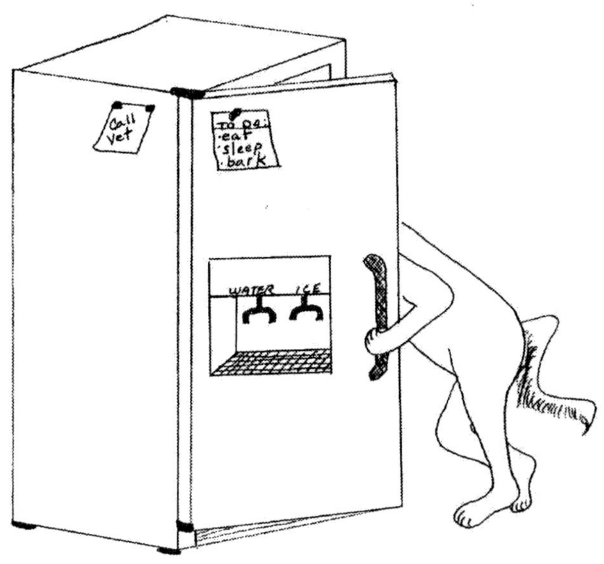

If revenge is sweet,
then where can I get some to eat?

There's more than one way to skin a cat,
but I'd never do a thing like that!

Always put your best foot forward
when standing on only three.

You "can" teach an old dog new tricks,
but the old ones are still the best.

I live to serve my master
which often results in disaster.

A fence is only as strong as its
weakest chain link.

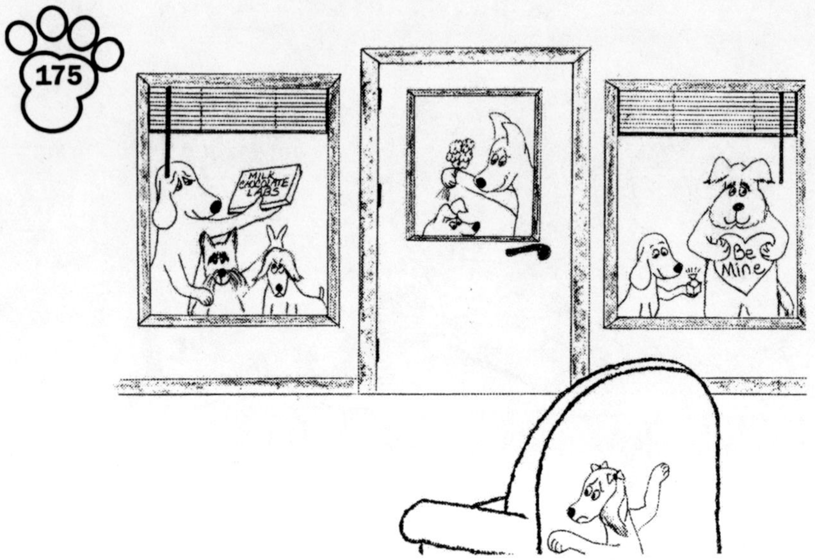

If you can't stand the heat, get spayed.

For a mongrel, variety is truly the spice of life.

While the cat's away it's fun to play with the mice.

Children should be seen but not heard or so it is said. That's kind of mean, but it would spare the pain in my head.

178

And now, a final word about some things I've SEEN and HEARD:

* A guide dog has seen what its master has only heard.
* When children are seen pulling tails, wails are heard.
* Attack dogs should be heard before they're seen.
* After a Pointer has seen the game, a shot is heard.
* Schnauzers can cause a scene and are almost always heard.
* With a muzzle, a master has seen to it that his dog's bark won't be heard.
* Dalmations are first on the scene when a siren is heard.
* Chihuahuas are heard but barely seen.
* Basenjis are seen but barely heard.
* A good watch dog has seen and heard everything.
* Dachshunds are seeeeeeeeeeeeeeeeeeeeeeeeeeeen.
* Sheep dogs herd.
* Puppies usually steal the scene.
* Dingos travel in a herd.
* Good dogs are seen obeying commands they've heard.
* I've heard that it's haughty to be seen with a Scottie.
* When a Rottweiler's teeth are seen, a scream may be heard.
* Hound dogs are seen chasing coons and heard baying at moons.
* Greyhounds are seen as a blur then sonic booms are heard.
* Dog whistles are seen but not heard by people.
* Invisible fences are heard but not seen by dogs.
* Fleas flee the scene as soon as they're seen.
* Cats are obscene and should never be seen or heard of again!

By now you've seen and heard it all.
I've nothing more to say.
Whenever you want to, give me a call
And I'll come and sit and stay
Again with you another day,
Then once more you can take a look
Inside my canine wisdom book.

Love and licks,

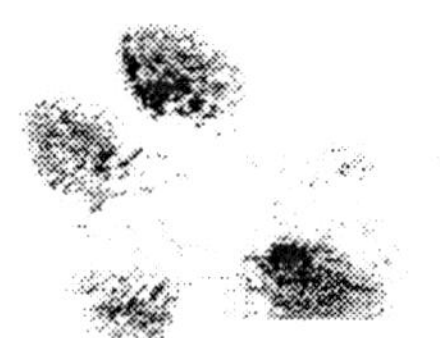

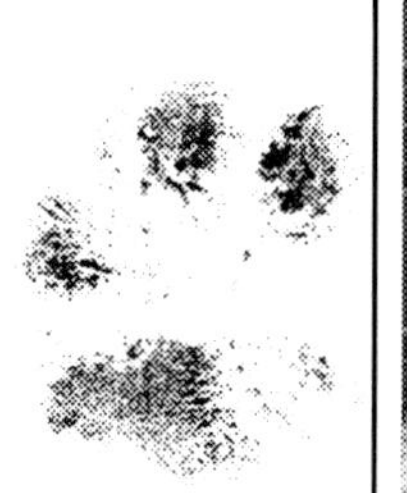

Index of Proverbs and Adages

2. A picture is worth a thousand words.
3. Clothes don't make the man.
4. Never put off until tomorrow what you can do today.
5. Don't bite the hand that feeds you.
6. The family that plays together stays together.
7. Seek and ye shall find.
8. He who laughs last laughs best.
9. A rolling stone gathers no moss.
10. Time flies when you're having fun.
11. A watched pot never boils.
12. Don't cry over spilled milk.
13. Love thy neighbor but don't pull down the hedge.
14. Desperate times call for desperate measures.
15. Beauty is only skin deep.
16. Blood is thicker than water.
17. Obey thy master.
18. A dog is man's best friend.
19. It's better to give than to receive.
20. A lie stands on one leg, truth on two.
21. To err is human; to forgive, divine.
22. Once bitten, twice shy.
23. When opportunity knocks, answer.
24. As you sow, so shall you reap.
25. One good deed deserves another.
26. An ounce of prevention is worth a pound of cure.
27. Don't burn your bridges behind you.
28. Time heals all wounds.
29. Catch as catch can.
30. Let thy discontents be secrets.
31. Early to bed, early to rise makes a man healthy, wealthy and wise.
32. One rotten apple can spoil the whole bunch.
33. An apple a day keeps the doctor away.
34. Eat, drink and be merry for tomorrow you may die.
35. It takes two to tango.
36. Better safe than sorry.
37. The grass is always greener on the other side of the fence.
38. If you lie down with dogs, you'll get up with fleas.

Index of Proverbs and Adages

39. Fools rush in where angels fear to tread.
40. A bird in the hand is worth two in the bush.
41. Two wrongs don't make a right.
42. Hitch your wagon to a star.
43. The squeaky wheel gets the grease.
44. Slow and steady wins the race.
45. If you live in a glass house don't throw stones.
46. Don't count your chickens until they're hatched.
47. The pen is mightier than the sword.
48. Silence is golden.
49. Fish and visitors stink after three days.
50. An idle brain is the Devil's workshop.
51. Spare the rod and spoil the child.
52. Sticks and stones may break my bones but words can never hurt me.
53. The way to a man's heart is through his stomach.
54. Turn about is fair play.
55. Lightning never strikes the same place twice.
56. All that glitters is gold.
57. Well done is better than well said.
58. Take time to smell the roses along the way.
59. Let sleeping dogs lie.
60. Eat to live not live to eat.
61. If the shoe fits, wear it.
62. Familiarity breeds contempt.
63. You can lead a horse to water but you cannot make him drink.
64. Leave no stone unturned.
65. The hand that rocks the cradle rules the world.
66. Out of the mouths of babes come crumbs.
67. The bigger they are the harder they fall.
68. The early bird catches the worm.
69. Two's company, three's a crowd.
70. Virtue is its own reward.
71. Feed a cold, starve a fever.
72. You are what you eat.
73. Curiosity killed the cat.
74. Walk softly and carry a big stick.
75. Cast not the first stone.
76. A rose by any other name smells the same.
77. Look before you leap.
78. Old habits die hard.
79. A card laid is a card played.

Index of Proverbs and Adages

80. Seeing is believing.
81. See no evil. Hear no evil. Speak no evil.
82. Birds of a feather flock together.
83. A friend in need is a friend indeed.
84. Don't stick your nose in someone else's business.
85. To thy own self be true.
86. There are plenty of fish in the sea.
87. Flattery will get you nowhere.
88. Out of sight, out of mind.
89. If you play with fire you'll get burned.
90. Strike while the iron is hot.
91. A word to the wise is sufficient.
92. Home is where the heart is.
93. A stitch in time saves nine.
94. Misery loves company.
95. Do as I say not as I do.
96. All's well that ends well.
97. Ask and ye may receive.
98. Actions speak louder than words.
99. Hell hath no fury like a woman scorned.
100. Beggars can't be choosers.
101. Better late than never.
102. No news is good news.
103. Many hands make light work.
104. Many are called, few are chosen.
105. Nice things come in small packages.
106. Walk a mile in my shoes.
107. There's no fool like an old fool.
108. The more the merrier.
109. If at first you don't succeed, try, try again.
110. It's always darkest before the dawn.
111. Practice what you preach.
112. All good things must come to an end.
113. Might makes right.
114. If you can't beat 'em, join 'em.
115. Charity begins at home.
116. March comes in like a lion and goes out like a lamb.
117. Don't put all your eggs in one basket.
118. A man is known by the company he keeps.
119. All work and no play makes Jack a dull boy.
120. Where there's a will there's a way.
121. Give a fellow enough rope and he'll hang himself.
122. There's a time and place for everything.

Index of Proverbs and Adages

123. Take things one step at a time.
124. The handwriting is on the wall.
125. Money is the root of all evil.
126. A dog's bark is worse than its bite.
127. He who hesitates is lost.
128. A woman's work is never done.
129. Practice makes perfect.
130. There's no time like the present.
131. A place for everything and everything in its place.
132. The golden rule: do unto others as you would have others do unto you.
133. A woman's place is in the home.
134. A leopard cannot change his spots.
135. Man cannot live by bread alone.
136. Accidents will happen.
137. One good turn deserves another.
138. Nothing ventured, nothing gained.
139. Different strokes for different folks.
140. Imitation is the sincerest form of flattery.
141. You can't have your cake and eat it too.
142. Two heads are better than one.
143. Hope springs eternal.
144. Too many cooks can spoil the pot.
145. Shape up or you'll be shipped out.
146. Honesty is the best policy.
147. Absence makes the heart grow fonder.
148. What goes around comes around.
149. Little strokes fell great oaks.
150. Haste makes waste.
151. Ignorance is bliss.
152. You never know what you can do until you try.
153. Hope for the best.
154. Like father, like son.
155. Great oaks from little acorns grow.
156. Between two stools one falls to the ground.
157. Experience is the best teacher.
158. Every man has his price.
159. Faith can move mountains.
160. Fight fire with fire.
161. Every dog has his day.
162. There's none so deaf as those who cannot hear.
163. What's bred in the bone comes out in the flesh.
164. Don't bite off more than you can chew.
165. Every rule has an exception.

Index of Proverbs and Adages

166. Give credit where credit is due.
167. Let the buyer beware.
168. Never give a sucker an even break.
169. Revenge is sweet.
170. There's more than one way to skin a cat.
171. Always put your best foot forward.
172. You can't teach an old dog new tricks.
173. He lives long who lives well.
174. A chain is only as strong as its weakest link.
175. If you can't stand the heat, get out of the kitchen.
176. Variety is the spice of life.
177. When the cat's away, the mice will play.
178. Children should be seen and not heard.

Pet Pages

If you've had a pet, you know how many cute, endearing, frustrating, tender or funny moments they can provide. Here's a place to record and recall those "special memories".

Pet Pages

Pet Pages

Do you need more copies of **Poor Tugger's Almanac** for friends and family?

Just complete and send this order form along with your check or money order to:

Poor Tugger Press
506 67th Street
Holmes Beach, FL 34217

Poor Tugger's Almanac of Canine Wisdoms

Proverbs...of the pooches, by the pooches, for the pooches

by Jolie Bell

Poor Tugger's Almanac of Canine Wisdoms is a humorous collection of familiar proverbs for adults but with a canine twist. Tugger, a precocious Miniature Schnauzer, fancies himself a four-footed, furry guru and shares with you some of his deepest and most profound thoughts. Great advice for the dog (or person) in your life!

PTP
POOR TUGGER PRESS

Order by mail with completed form along with check or money order to:
Poor Tugger Press
506 67th Street
Holmes Beach, FL 34217

No. of Books: ______________ x $14.95
Shipping: $______________ ($2.95/book)
Total: $______________

Name: ______________________ Address: ______________________

City: ____________ State: ____________ Zip: ____________ Phone: ____________

Your e-mail address: ______________________________________

For additional information please e-mail: *poortuggerpress@aol.com*

Printed in the United States
39244LVS00011B/409-597